MW01154716

This book belongs to

_____

I was laying on the floor of the treehouse when
Problem Solving Ninja popped in.

A painting set was starting to ooze paint onto the wooden floorboard. I had gotten upset when the painting hadn't come out right.

Jigsaw puzzles, rocket activities, card games – all of them laid messily across the floor. I had only started the rocket activity, but had gotten bored and stopped.

Of course, you can.
No, I can't. Otherwise, I would have done it already.

The 4 Ps

Passion - means wanting to do something.
Purpose - means having a reason for doing it.
Plan - means working out how to do it.
Positivity - so you keep trying until you get it right!

That evening, I asked for some tips on knitting.

Then, I set a plan to practice just ten minutes a day.

A few weeks later, when it was my Grandma's birthday, I gave her the present.

She held up a beautiful long scarf and a woolly beanie hat with a pom-pom on top of it.

She put them on straight away, even though it was a warm day, and told everyone that I had made them for her!

Remembering the 4 Ps could be your secret weapon in building your motivation superpower!

Visit ninjalifehacks.tv for your Ninja Rocket Template.

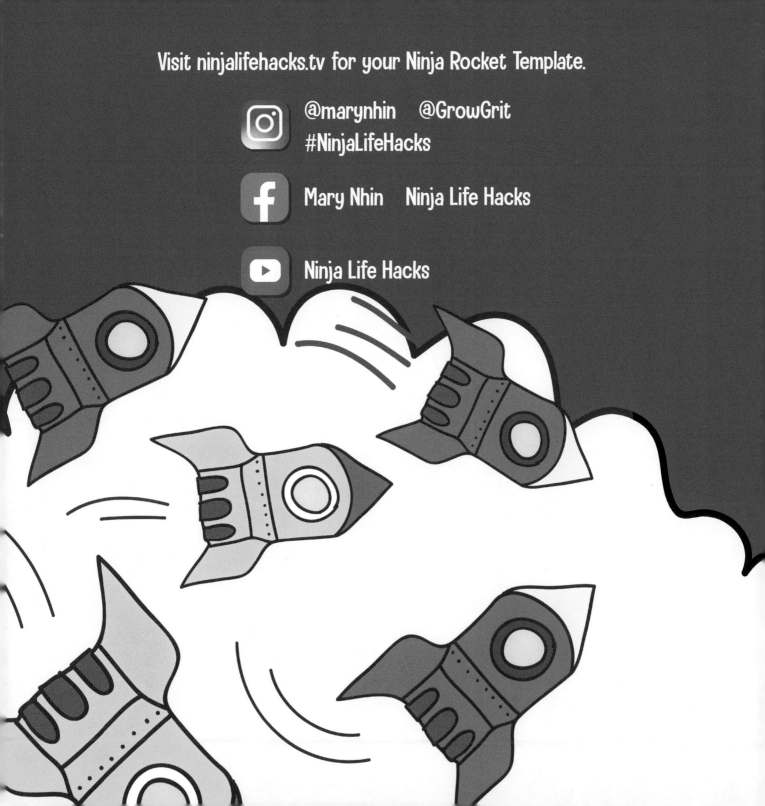

@marynhin   @GrowGrit
#NinjaLifeHacks

Mary Nhin   Ninja Life Hacks

Ninja Life Hacks

CPSIA information can be obtained
at www.ICGtesting.com
Printed in the USA
BVHW022127200622
640271BV00004B/28